FUN ACTIVITIES TO DO WITH YOUR KIDS

INCLUDES 50 FUN THINGS TO DO FOR
PARENTS AND CHILDREN

JENNIFER LOVE

CONTENTS

1. Explore, Learn, and Have Fun!   1
2. Fun Indoors   5
3. Outdoor Excitement   11
4. Be Creative, Design, and Experiment   17
5. Awesome Fun Family Get-togethers   23

Afterword   27

1

EXPLORE, LEARN, AND HAVE FUN!

Every human being is blessed to have five primary senses - sight, hearing, smell, touch and taste. These senses are not yet fully developed at birth. A very good example of this is your sense of sight.

Have you ever wondered why babies love colorful rattles? This is because their eyes cannot fully distinguish colors yet and can only perceive bright colors. You may have also thought that your kid can already recognize or see you during his infancy period. The truth is that infants can only perceive shadows at this age.

On the other hand, one of the senses that are already developed at the time of birth is hearing. This primary sense is said to be first one to develop; in fact, it can already develop while the fetus is inside the womb of his mother. Out of the five primary senses, hearing is also said to be the last one to perish in the face of death. In fact, research shows that it can even persist a few hours after death.

What is the significance of these primary senses in the growth and development of your child? These senses are not just important in the survival of the child and appreciation of his surroundings; they are also essential in your kid's learning process. How he learns the alphabet, the colors and the numbers are all influenced by his senses of sight, hearing, taste, smell and touch.

Every child undergoes several stages of learning and development. Each learning stage is associated with a certain learning technique or style that the child utilizes in order to facilitate his cognitive and physical maturation. For example, a toddler who still cannot read a book or even memorize the names of objects would most likely recognize different items through his senses of smell, vision and taste. You might have already seen a child who seems to be very fond of putting everything into his mouth, with no regard to whether the object is edible or not. This is because the child tries to familiarize himself with the object by tasting it. You might have also noticed some children who do not want to eat green apples but love eating the red ones. This is because they can only recognize the red apple, but not the green one.

Toddlerhood is also the stage during which the child seeks to exhibit his autonomy. How does this happen? Have you ever seen your child say "yes" to the things that you say? Or is it more likely that he does not want to eat, he does not want to take a bath, and he does not want you to help him assemble his toys? If he answers no every time you offer to help, then he is positively undergoing toddlerhood.

You might have interpreted this as stubbornness, but the truth is, it is a toddler's nature to be negativistic. When this happens, it is helpful if you let him do what he wants. Exploration is one of the ways that toddlers can learn. Let him dance in the rain and let him play with mud all he wants. There is one thing that you should do at this stage, though, and that is to keep him safe.

When your child reaches the age of six, he will most likely learn through storytelling. Preschool stage is the period during which the imagination of a kid starts to widen. You might have already heard your kid telling you about his imaginary friend or his exaggerated stories about how he incurred a wound on his elbow when he was playing with his ball. During this period, you might worry that your child is hallucinating or is delusional. He is not. His horizon and vocabulary are just starting to expand. The best way to optimize your child's learning during this stage is to let him play with his siblings or neighbors of the same age as his, and to tell him more stories that can challenge his imagination. Reading him a bedtime story every night is one way of helping him learn at this stage.

Your child then soon reaches school age, the stage at which your child can effectively learn from classroom activities, teachers and classmates. His learning style will again take another turn, as he can now read and write the alphabet.

The learning process does not stop there; rather, it continues into adult life. As the child grows older, he starts to make use of other modalities to learn, which include games, crafts and other activities. He also starts to shift his focus from himself to the people around him. His activities that start from solitary plays in infancy and parallel plays in toddlerhood become more interactive with the involvement of his friends. He participates in associative types of play at preschool, cooperative play at school age, and competitive play at adolescence. Along with the evolution of his activities, he becomes more responsible of his obligations, especially with role-playing games. He learns to obey the rules of the game, and later on, universal laws, and he enhances his decision-making skills.

But as learning and development take place, it is also essential that you stay with him all throughout his growing years. Guidance and wisdom are some of the best things that you can impart as he starts to gain control of his surroundings. Everything that you show and tell him is critical to his physical, mental, social and emotional development. At this point, your child needs a role model whom he can identify himself with. Be that role model who will lead your child to the right path. Spend more time with him, play with him, support him in his activities at school and help him overcome difficulties that he may experience during this stage.

Having fun is a vital part of the maturation process and your child needs it, too. Aside from watching TV and playing with his toys, what else can your child do to learn while also having fun at the same time? Flip on the page and find out 50 things that your child can do with or without you.

2

FUN INDOORS

Heavy rain, cold snow, or too much heat from the sun; these are just some of the things that can hinder your child from exploring the outside world and encourage him to stay in the comfort of his own home instead. You might think that staying indoors would be very boring for your child, but the truth is, there are a lot of fun activities that your child can do at home.

The good thing about staying indoors is that you get to supervise your child more closely. The threats of accidents, injuries and diseases are also reduced, as your home provides effective protection against harmful external elements. Whatever the weather, let your child learn while having a good time doing these great indoor activities!

1. Fort Building

One of the classic indoor activities that children play is fort building, an activity where the kids make a castle or a house using furniture, toys, blankets, pillows and other objects they lay their eyes on. This activity is much better played with 3 or more kids. Anticipate their room to be in chaos afterwards, but also expect to see your kids playing all day long. In their make-believe castle, they can do a lot of fun things, such as taking on the role of kings and queens, playing with their stuffed toys and pretending to be soldiers fighting with their swords.

1. **Get Board Games on Board**

There are many board games that kids can play nowadays. Board games can be as simple as Snakes and Ladders, or as educational as Scrabble, or as strategic as chess. Board games are better played with siblings and friends. You can also play with your children, mentoring and supervising them at the same time. Teach them how to invest or use their money with Monopoly, or teach them how to form words out of different letters with Scrabble. Playing board games, whether it rains or shines, is a fun way to spend one awesome day with your kids at home.

1. **Watch a Movie**

A classic way of spending a winter night with your kids is watching a movie that your kids love. Choose from various animated movies, comedy films and inspirational movies, prepare a bowl of cheese-flavored popcorn, huddle up inside your blankets, and lay yourself comfortably on the couch as you turn your living room into a cozy, dark movie theatre. Laugh, be thrilled, scream and cry with your kids. On a cold winter night, sit back, relax and enjoy the film!

1. **Disco Fever**

Turn any room in your house into a dance floor as you turn up the music and groove to the beat. Have some fun with your kids through this very exhausting but absolutely healthy activity. If you and your kids have not done any exercise for the past few days, then a dance party can be a great alternative. This activity not only promotes the health of your kids, but also enhances the coordination of their body parts. With better coordination, they are more able to maintain balance, which can help them prevent injuries and falls in the future. Dancing is also another way of fighting stress. Though your kids may not feel any anxiety at the present, dancing helps uplift their spirit, thus allowing them to fight off stressful situations.

1. **Like the Pirates of the Caribbean**

Your kids will surely love this simple game of treasure hunting. Look for a spot in your house where you can hide little rewards like candies, chocolates, or the toy they have been raving about. You can add a twist to your little treasure hunting activity by giving them a treasure map. Draw a map of your house and indicate the location of the treasure with a cute symbol. Let your kids enjoy acting like pirates, dress them in black robes and black hats, and give them their magical telescope. This will definitely keep your kids engrossed in their play all day long.

1. **Act it out!**

Best played by three or more children, this game will not just keep your kids laughing but it will also keep your kids thinking and guessing! The first thing that you have to do is to prepare the items or the topics that the players will have to act out and guess. Remember to limit the topics to things that the kids know; it can be the cartoon characters they love most or the title of their favorite nursery rhyme. Then, divide the players into two teams. Each team will have to assign a player to act out the item picked while the rest of the team deciphers what is being presented. Exaggerate your movements to make this game even better!

1. **Bathroom Games**

The bathroom is one of the most common places where children play. This is where they make and blow bubbles, where they play with the shower, and where they can play with their toys. Turn your bathtub into a playground. For your little girls, teach them the concept of responsibility by letting them bathe their Barbie dolls. On the other hand, your little boys will most likely play with your razors and toothbrushes. Let them stand in front of a mirror and act like grown-up men. That would really be a sight to behold! But because the bathroom is also one of the most hazardous places at home, it is better that you stay with them all throughout their bathroom play. Be cautious, for they might slip, drown or fall while playing.

1. **Puppet Shows.**

Many kids love watching puppet shows in theaters. However, for this activity, let them do the acting and you the watching. Gather your kids up in the living room for a fun puppet-making time. Look for hand-me-down clothes, art materials like strings and colored papers, and old socks in your closets that can be used to make the puppets. The best part of this activity is that your kids get to learn how to be imaginative while creating their own puppets. You can also make use of their dolls and stuffed toys. The next thing to do is to prepare the stage of the puppet show. Hang a blanket or a curtain across your living room, high enough to hide your kids in the backstage. Sit back and relax as you watch how your kids' made-up story turns out in the end.

1. **Indoor Miniature Golf.**

Golf is a great outdoor activity for your kids. However, when the rain is pouring or when the snow is so heavy that you don't have any choice but to stay inside your home, you'll find that golf is also a fun indoor activity. You can get a mini golf set in thrift stores, or you can make use of the materials you have at home. If you don't have a mini golf set yet, here's what you can do: first, you have to find a golf ball. Ping-pong balls, stress balls or a small rubber balls will also do. Just make sure that the object that you are going to use is not made of glass to prevent injuries. Next, look for something that you can use as a golf club. This is an easier task. Your broom can be a perfect alternative, or any wooden stick that you can find. Now the only thing that is lacking is the hole on the golf course. No fuss. You can make use of a plastic cup for this.

1. **Make Chores Fun.**

Doing some household chores is one of the most productive ways your kids can spend their time. Not only that! Getting them working on some household chores, like washing dishes or sweeping the floor, turns them into responsible kids. Teach them the concept of obligation and give them the chance to feel a sense of achievement. You can work with your daughter in the kitchen, letting her mix your baking ingredients or asking her to wash her spoon and fork. On the other hand, you can teach the sense of responsibility to your son by asking him to fix all his toys in his cabinet.

3

OUTDOOR EXCITEMENT

Childhood will not be complete without a fun-filled trip to the zoo, an exhausting game of football, and the excitement of playing hide and seek. Remember when you were young and your mom just kept on calling your name from the house, telling you to stop playing, change your clothes and eat? Or how you were drenched in sweat because you have been playing in the sun for a few hours or so? These are the days that you won't surely forget, right? And so, these are the days that you want your kids to experience as well.

Give your kids a break from errands and the demands of school. Whether it be summer or winter, let them explore the outdoors. Give them the chance to feel the warmth of the summer sun or the chilly breeze of winter. After all, being a kid is all about exploration, learning and having fun!

Here are some great outdoor activities that you can try with your kids:

1. **Scrabble with a Twist**

Who says that Scrabble is a boring board game? Well, here is some good news! You can turn the traditional game of Scrabble into an amazing outdoor game. Plus, as much as 5 or more kids, including you, can participate in this outdoor Scrabble. Prepare a set of alphabet flashcards patterned after your Scrabble tiles and put them in a large container. Then, look for a spot in your garden or front lawn where you can play. Ideally, the area should be big enough to accommodate 15 letters vertically and horizontally. Have your kids pick seven letters at a time and instruct them not to show these letters to anyone. When everyone is ready, or when you have already decided who will go first, then you can start your outdoor Scrabble game.

1. **Glowing Bowling**

Ever heard of glow-in-the-dark bowling pins? Night bowling will definitely be a lot of fun, and your kids will absolutely go frenzy over this unique activity. If you don't have glow-in-the-dark pins, you can actually make them at home. All you need are ten empty plastic bottles and ten glowing camp sticks of various colors. Any type of ball will do for the bowling ball, whether it be a basketball, a volleyball or a football. All you have to do is place your camp sticks inside these plastic bottles and go out into your backyard. And poof! You have instant glow-in-the-dark bowling pins. Set these pins around 5 meters away from you and let your kid bowl a strike!

1. **Fly a Kite**

Most people regard kite-flying as a boring activity. You stay in one place, hold your string up and look up at the sky.

However, flying a kite with your kids can be a one-of-a-kind experience. Start this exciting activity by helping your kids create their own kites. Prepare art materials of different colors and shapes, as well as sticks and adhesives for the frame of the kite. Run around the park as you fly your kite as high as you can.

1. **Climb a Tree**

Kids are natural adventure-seekers, and one of the most popular and exciting outdoor activities that they do is to climb a tree. Some kids even build their own tree house and build their blanket forts high above the tree. However, this activity is, of course, not recommended for kids under the age of five, since their gross motor functions are not that well-developed yet. Help them build a treehouse, join their genius role-play and enjoy the view of the neighborhood from the top.

1. **Paint, Paint, Paint**

If you have an old tarpaulin in storage or posters that you are no longer using, then you can donate these to your kids for their art-making project. Lay the old posters on your lawn, together with paints and brushes, and let your kid do the mixing and matching of colors. This activity does not just take the boredom away, but it can also be an educational activity for your child. Encourage him or her to use primary colors, such as red, yellow and blue, and let him or her discover that mixing them produces secondary colors.

1. **Hide and Seek**

One classic outdoor game is hide and seek. Surely, every kid in town loves playing this game. Give it a twist by playing sardines, which is reversed hide and seek, where the "it" is the first to hide. He will then be sought by the next "it" who will also hide with him. This goes on until only one player is left and all of them get stuck in the same place like a can of sardines!

1. **Jump on a Trampoline**

Kids and adults alike love to jump on a trampoline. Set your trampoline at the middle of your lawn and invite as many kids into the playing area. Join the mob and jump as high as you can!

1. **Build a Snowman**

Nothing to do this snowy winter? Well, here is one activity that you and your kids will truly enjoy. As snow builds up on your driveway, grab this golden opportunity to bond with your kids. Take them out, but of course with the appropriate attire, and let them make balls of snow with their little hands. To make a bigger snowball, roll the small ones in the snow. Don't forget to decorate the snowman with a red scarf and sticks for arms.

1. **Dodge Ball**

One of the most exciting games of all time! This game is better played with five or more kids. You can serve as the referee while the kids play. Basically, the players are split into two teams. Choose the team that will throw the ball, also called the "it" team, and the team that will try to avoid being hit by the ball. The player who gets hit by the ball is out, while the player who gets to catch it stays in the game. The other team gets to play "it" once all the members of the other team are eliminated.

1. **Tag**

This is another classic outdoor game that all kids play. Call all the kids in the neighbourhood and choose an "it" from among them. The "it" tries to tag someone while the rest of the kids run around, trying to avoid being tagged. The tagged player freezes and stays in that position until another untagged kid tags him.

1. **Take Your Dog out for Some Scavenger Hunting**

Your dogs need as much exercise as you do, and there is no better way to keep them healthy than letting them running around with your kids. Take them out into your front lawn and let them search for something, most usually a bone that you have thrown.

1. **Wash the Family Car**

After a hard day's work, you are probably too tired to wash your car. Make car washing fun as you call your kids to help you out. Watch as your kids play with the bubbles and have with a good time splashing in the water.

1. **Sing and Dance in the Rain**

Don't let the rain spoil your kids' day. Set your fears

aside for now and let your kids enjoy the free shower. Just make sure to bathe them with soap and clean water and dry them up thoroughly afterwards to prevent them from catching a cold.

1. **Play Jump Rope**

Give your kids the chance to develop their jumping skills and let them play with their jumping ropes! Give this simple activity a twist by dividing them into two teams. Each team must form a line and compete to reach the end of the lawn, using their jumping ropes. The team to finish first wins and gets a prize!

1. **Water Gun Fight**

Act like action stars with your water guns. Equip each of your children with a water gun, then let them hide and hunt each other out. The last one standing wins!

4
BE CREATIVE, DESIGN, AND EXPERIMENT

One of the ways a child learns is by getting dirty and stinky. It is part of every child's adventure-seeking behavior, and it is your role as the parent to guide your children through these activities and not to stop them from having these experiences.

Here are some simple activities that you can do with your kids to facilitate their learning and development.

1. Complete a Jigsaw Puzzle

Every individual must have solved a jigsaw puzzle or two at some point in their lives. There are jigsaw puzzles that are easy, difficult, and sometimes, extremely difficult to solve. Guide your kid as he tries to complete the missing pieces of the puzzle. This is not just a fun way of spending one's free time, but it also enhances your child's memory and cognition.

1. Read a Book

As young as they are, children should already be taught how to read and listen well. The development of these mental functions is enhanced by letting them read a storybook and listen to an audio version. You can also read them their most favorite bedtime story to help them with their language skills.

1. **Organize a Garage Art Show**

Kids are artistic and creative in nature, and what better way to hone their artistic talents than to let them exhibit their art works to a crowd? Turn your garage into an art gallery and invite other kids in. Not only will this develop your child's inner artistic potential, but it will also boost his self-confidence.

1. **Artificially Color Flowers**

Time for a little experiment in the backyard. Be surprised by how a white flower turns into unique shades of purple, orange, yellow and red. You will need a white rose, or any flower for that matter, a dye or a food coloring (choose whatever color your kids love), and a jar of water. To do this, dissolve or mix the dye or food coloring into the water. Cut the stem of the flower from its main trunk and dip it into the colored water. Set this aside overnight. Check your flower the next day to see the color change.

1. **Plant a Seed**

Teach your kids how to be an environment-friendly person. Prepare a fruit seed and let him plant it in your backyard. Stay with him as he plants it so that you can walk him through the process. Ask him to water it afterwards.

1. **Flashcards Night**

Nothing to do tonight? Well, this could be the perfect activity for your preschool child. Prepare two sets of flashcards- one set made up of numbers ranging from 1 to 10, while the other set contains a picture of objects in varying amounts. Let your kids hold the number set while you hold the picture set. As you hold out one flashcard at a time, ask your kids to hold out the flashcard containing the number that corresponds to the picture shown.

1. **Butt Spell**

Give the traditional name-spelling a twist by letting your kids spell their names with their butts. You will surely laugh out loud with your kids in this entertaining spelling activity.

1. **Alphabet Matchup**

With your kids, mere recitation of alphabets may not be enough. Take their alphabet learning experience to a higher level by encouraging them to say a word that starts with the alphabet they have been given. You can choose a category per round; for example, the first round can be all about fruits. Ask them to identify a fruit that starts with the letter "A" and so on.

1. **Make a Hot Air Balloon**

Your kids will surely enjoy this little scientific experiment. Get an empty glass bottle and cover its lid with the opening of a deflated balloon. Over a basin of hot water, let the glass bottle float and see what happens. If done correctly, the balloon will expand as the air inside it starts to get warm. As it heats up, the air molecules begin to move away from one another, causing the expansion of the balloon.

1. The Ultimate Paper Boat

Most kids make paper boats that only last for a few minutes on the water. For a more lasting activity, let your kids make this water-resistant paper boat. All you need are few sheets of cartons and rolls of masking and scotch tapes. First, help your kids make the boat out of the cartons that you have. Second, cover these paper boats with a lot of tape to ensure its durability. Let it float onto the water and see if it sinks.

1. Tic-Tac-Toe

Enjoy this well-known indoor game with your kids and enhance their strategic skills. To make it more fun, instead of using a pen, you can use big flashcards with X's and O's on them; instead of using paper, utilize your front lawn.

1. Go Stargazing

One of the most exciting night activities ever! Lay down with your kids in your backyard and wait for meteors to come crashing down the night sky. Give them some background about the stars, the moon and the other planets, and introduce them to Big Dipper, Cassiopeia, Gemini and other constellations.

1. **Magnifying Lenses and the Sun**

Let your kid act like a little detective in this simple experiment. You will need a magnifying glass, a piece of paper or dry leaf, and the heat of the sun. This experiment involves the formation of a small fire; thus, your watchful guidance is recommended. First, look for a safe spot in your backyard where the risk of the fire spreading is minimal, such as a cemented area. Set your paper or dry leaf on this area and directly hold the magnifying glass over the paper. Focus the rays of the sun on this glass until you see a small dot of the sun's light on the paper. Wait for a few moments and witness your paper get burned!

1. **Painting Stones**

Your kids must love collecting different items from the environment- stones, leaves and other objects that you might think are not at all useful. Teach your kids the concept of recycling by turning a grey stone into a colorful paper weight. Gather your painting materials and let your kid decorate her stones.

1. **Say Thank You with a Card**

Teaching a kid how to say thank you is one of the most important tasks that you have to do as a parent. Help her unleash her creativity, and at the same time, teach her the importance of saying thank you by letting her make her own thank you card. Encourage her to give this card to someone she is most thankful to.

5

AWESOME FUN FAMILY GET-TOGETHERS

One of the best gifts that you can give your children is your precious time. Spending some moments with them, especially during the weekends, is a great way of showing your love for them. Whether you take a trip out or you stay at home all day long, what matters is that you are there for them every step of the way.

Here are some fun activities that you can do with your kids during your family bonding time!

1. Go on a Picnic

What's a better way to spend a sunny afternoon than to go on a picnic? Enjoy the scenery, the fresh air, the good food, and of course, the good times in this outdoor activity.

1. Camp in Your Own Backyard

If there's a will, there's a way. If time and the demands of your job are preventing you from taking an out-of-town trip with your kids, then you can go out to your lawn, build a tent under the moonlight and set up a bonfire. Complete your backyard camping experience with some grilled hotdogs and roasted marshmallows.

1. **Bake**

Most children, and especially girls, love watching their mom in the kitchen. Why not make it more fun for them by letting them participate? Ask them to break and beat some eggs and mix some flour and sugar. This will be one of their most memorable moments ever!

1. **Build a House for Their Puppy**

Teach your kids how to hold a hammer and a nail as you build a house for the family puppy. Let them participate by asking them how they want the kennel to look like, what color to use and what materials to use. This improves their decision-making skills.

1. **Explore the Neighbourhood**

Act like a tourist in your own town or city by visiting some of its most beautiful places. Take a walk in the park, plunge into the swimming pool of a nearby resort or visit the herbarium.

1. **Go to an Amusement Park**

Take your kids to the nearest amusement park and enjoy all day long. Watch as your kids are fascinated by the giant Ferris wheel and hear them scream on a roller-coaster ride.

1. **Get an Ice Cream Cone**

Whether it is a sunny or a rainy day, ice cream will always be one of your kid's favorites. Buy a gallon of their favorite ice cream flavor and enjoy it with your children as you all watch their choice of cartoons.

1. **Take a Trip to the Zoo**

Go on a field trip with your kids and take them to the zoo. Show them the lions, tigers, snakes, elephants and other animals. You can also let them feed the giraffe with grass to make their experience more memorable.

1. **Do Some Gardening**

Your kids must really be curious about how plants grow and produce fruits. Teach them some basics by letting them garden with you. Let them weed out some grasses and water the plants. They will surely love wearing a pair of those gardening gloves that you have.

1. **Form Something out of Dominoes**

Put your kids' ability to concentrate to a test by giving them this task. Using a box of dominoes, ask your kids to form letters and write their names on your driveway. Make sure that each letter is connected to the next. Afterwards, ask your kid to tap on the last piece of domino making up the last letter of his name. Watch how the dominoes fall in a series.

AFTERWORD

Exploring new places, making discoveries and meeting new faces are just some of the ways your kids can learn and have fun at the same time. With these 50 activities, your kids can say goodbye to boring moments and say hello to fun and enjoyment.

Thank you for reading and I hope you enjoyed this resource!

www.ingramcontent.com/pod-product-compliance
Lightning Source LLC
Chambersburg PA
CBHW052130110526
44592CB00013B/1819